SOFT LAUNCH

CONTENTS

ONE

ZERO

CODA

SOFT LAUNCH

Spray Tans

I'm either not as good at being
who I think I am, or I'm way better—
so much so that I almost no longer
recognize the person I once was
as being connected, via the present,
to the man I hope, one day, to be.
And if that's the case, either

neither are you or so are you
but even more so. It's a matter
of degrees—and also of Degree
Dry Protection Antiperspirant
Deodorant, and maybe also of Attilio
Degrassi, Italian scholar of Latin
epigraphy. No, I threw that last

one in as an example of a false
positive. One mustn't simply
assume one's beta virgin, pimply
and spry, can step naturally into
the rainbows of tomorrowland!
One's too familiar with sorrow, and
one doesn't enjoy *time*, per se.

At least not what it does to May
or to its moons as it lapses,
however confidently, into false June.
What I'm saying, however clunkily,
is that I resent the way time redacts
its many months, however funkily,
giving rise to a lone apocalypse

of singular sun and million Satans
springing for—well, spray tans,
let's be honest. They don't call it
the Yellow Devil for nothing.
They don't call it "Honey Darling"
for no reason at all. It's
because they got it at the mall.

A Request

Hey, u want to lend me some of your crap

I don't have enough crap

everywhere

Thankfully

I have a friend who knows
a little something about everything
and is, thankfully, willing to add
his two cents to every conversation.

"My narwhal's misbehaving," I
mutter one day. "Ah," he chimes in,
"Have you tried jiggling its tusk?"
He has owned several narwhals

and been to a number of shows.
His familiarity with titles
is unmatched: "Have you read
Escape from Jeff the Killer yet?"

When I suggest it is a Minecraft
map he tilts his head and smiles:
"It's also a book by Will Schofield,
limited edition from Leaf Storm Press."

I have a friend who loves food
so much there's nothing he hasn't
prepared for every type of eater.
"Borscht for toddlers? Add beetroot,"

he says, "Strange as that may sound."
"What about for Peruvian toddlers,"
I ask. "Try wheat germ," he suggests,
and hops in a small blue Honda

from which blue smoke belches
as he drives off toward JC Penney
to return a 12-inch classic satchel
assembled from royal claret leather.

Very Brave

This poem is about you.
You assume I mean someone else,
which is fine.

You remind me of a skyscraper,
or rather the lost plans
for one. The architect, too,
has been lost—abducted, maybe.

Or she got bored and faked her own death.
Her name was Beth, I think.
She was gay, and
she was very brave, they say.

This poem is not about
losing door keys and coming to terms
with it (lol, Marianne)—

nor is it about losing the big game,
stepping barefoot on a pottery shard,
changing one's own name
or coming up short in some other regard.

This poem is about you being you,
sitting there, full of unwarranted guilt,
like a gift card unspent
or a building unbuilt.

Love Poem

You are lipstick
on the Starbucks lid
in the trashcan
of my life.

Grocery Sonnet

As at the grocer's she held up a Manwich
box and said "You should buy this
because you're a *man*," and I said so
should you because you're a *wich*.
So also she pointed to the bratwurst
and said, "or that, because you're a *brat*,"
and I said so should you, you're the *wurst*.
She held up a frankfurter and said I
should buy it because my name is *Frank*
and I said no you should because you're
furtive. She said that doesn't make sense,
and I said neither does your mom.
She skulked slyly out the side door,
and I never heard from her no more.

Against One Odd

Our love persists against
not all odds but certain odds.
Okay, one odd: your odd brother
who still wets his propeller
beanie. Okay, and doesn't know
how to wear a beanie.
Or shall we say *where*. And should
I call your brother an "odd"
even in an effort to get even
with your odd family, you being
one of five, with your bright
eyes and silly haircut,
you still want me to wash dishes.
You still want me to mow yard,
to pull weeds and skim pool.
Our love persists despite
a baffling headwind
and that we are still chased
by nude firemen everywhere.
Perhaps I should forgive myself
for releasing the nude firemen
from their holding cell.
Or try. It hasn't been easy.

Love Poem

If you, eternal love, lapse
into nonsense often,
it is because words can't contain
your wiseacre ideas; and
the only way you could be so
self-consciously unattractive
is if you have, as you claim,
thoroughly rejected beauty
in favor of a much larger
and saggier pair of
ideals: Courage and Despair.
Feels good to be queen
of this corner of town,
doesn't it? What of that Wrangler
jacket, the winter nicotine
wafting from your skin,
exposed legs white, wreathed
in varicosity so ferocious only
a warlock could untangle it,
and even he would need props
from whomever was watching.
Let's keep our fingers crossed,
fellow terrestrial, wee harpist
on my heart-strings,
promoter of odd events, & well-
attended, clear-eyed sergeant
of both of our fortunes.
And our legs and eyes, all crossed
lest our bodies, beset, begin
to ache: Crossed for lack
of access's sake.

Lovesong

How dumb are you? Well, let's see.
Let's start with how dumb I am,
and I can answer that simply

by pointing to my garden.
It's fruitful. I'm not dumb,
nor, despite your fondness of me,

are you. You're brilliant, sweet;
if the world's a vegetable stew
you are its best little pea,

and I mean that sincerely.
I don't love stew, Marjorie.
Maybe I'm good not with words,

but then again neither are you,
I'd wager, based on your verbal.
Oh, you don't like bringing

that up? Haha, math whiz.
You auto-outperform a quadratic
equation scholar in your *head*

but don't know where Bath is.
You know where the bath is,
and so do I. So do *we*. How cute

are we, padding from the *en suite*
all damp and betowelled? Well
I'll leave that to the crowd

to determine by its applause.
Meanwhile we'll be in the loveseat
kissing and trading old saws.

Pivots Into Wildness

No one but Spock and God
are entirely or even
mostly rational. No one
but you and I are entirely
or even half irrational.

And yet I should say,
I'd rather you be you,
mistaking some things
for things that they aren't,
than you be me, seeing

everything in squares
or arranged along lines.
But I'd rather me be me,
not allowing incompatible
categories to overlap,

than me be you, assuming
buying a vacuum cleaner
means pitching the broom.
I guess one might file this
under the dreaded "you do

you, boo," but I'd rather
think of it as ontological,
à la Popeye's *I am what I am*
followed by the caveat
and that's all that I am.

But is this all that *we* are?
No concession of weakness,
an acknowledgement
that the self has a limit
explains, in part, our penchant

for boiled kale and beets.
We build ourselves up
to make ourselves stronger
in body if not in mind,
leave the weird stuff behind.

My Space

So this girl messages me
do you want to hang out sometime.
So I look and see she actually has a boyfriend.
The boyfriend as it turns out is a reindeer.
And not only that, a metal display reindeer.
He has a brassiere tangled around one of his antlers.
One of his eyes is missing.
He says to me, "Man?"
Followed by long silence.
I look over my shoulder to see if anyone's coming.
"What you doin' messin' with my princess."
Just like that.
Like I had even messaged her back.
Then he begins to cough and I can see
he's coughing blood onto the carpet.
It's not much blood but the basement
of my aunt's house is the wrong place for this.
I should have paid attention in school.
I should have gone to Russia.
I shouldn't have skipped cross country.
This girl messages me again
this time just three dots.
Like I should have replied already.
But I know I'll never really *have it all*.
I look and see that she's no longer online.
And not only that, her profile is gone.
A man comes in and asks me about the reindeer.
I say I didn't do anything, he just started coughing.
The man says this never happened, you weren't here.
I realize nothing ever really happens.
But I miss her already and we've never met.

TWO

A Marketer's Prayer

Lord, let me deliver key capabilities
but not within one segment:
across the entire demographic.

Poet In The World

Jesus, must I
always be munching
the nether teats
of Corporate America?
Must I always be
a floundering
foundling?
Or will the brights
of your grace fix
my hooves in
place, both
my clicking hooves
and my cloven?
Maybe I'm too hard
to pin down, God,
or to make much of—
maybe too doe-eyed
or doughy.

Witch Hunt

Some witch-hunts
discover real witches,

so they aren't witch-hunts
in the idiomatic sense
but rather an identification

and uprooting of evil,
tall, merciless people

who've traded their thinking caps
for towering hats of magic,

who now slather, eyes dilated,
wandering forlornly
along the far edge of some unlucky
farmer's field, seeking

whom best to devour
this fine Friday afternoon

as if a mob weren't en route,
a witch-hunting crew with torches,
even in the daylight,

and pitchforks,
even though John Deere equipment
is parked where it's supposed to be parked.

"We will find and burn you,"
they say in monotone, in unison;

"We will light you up."

Calf Ink Line

Nothing comes between
me and my cave-ins.

Nothing beats Ween
on a hot Bonderday night

as the double moon
rises from its awful
stall in the West.

Calves, moseying in and out
as your phone blinkers
and tanks, its witch-switch
broken, obviously.

"If the lion's
distracting, den him,"
zoologists caution.

Den him. But how?
Leathery frills? Stonewashed?

"Ah, farm life," you maybe muse.

"Freak you," I chortlingly shoot back.

Outrage

I threw up my hands in disgust:
Why had I eaten my hands?

B Positive

Got into an accident
with a teenager

& was bleeding a lot.
I need blood,

I told her.
Am I your type,

she asked.
I'm B positive,

what are you?
O totally, she said.

Chastened

My squid no longer works.
It missed brunch. It's heart-broken.
Nor does my harbinger
function properly; it fails to point
furtively toward future gloom.
It points backward to shows
one shouldn't have attended
and those one shouldn't have attended
them with. It points upward to God
(*god-ward*).
       John
William Godward, Victorian
Neoclassicist painter of
some repute. Some ill repute,
that is: "Big Dreamer" Godward
saw everything in colourful
haze. My aunt Caki Wilkinson
no longer works as it was designed
to work, as well. It was to
summon not books but slight
lyrics, mere shadows; it has come on
full-tilt as they used to say.

My stevedore collection, finally,
isn't "broken," but parts of it
are missing, so yeah
that's another thing that's effed
in my life. Welcome to my world,
creeper. Why are you reading this?

The Black Prince

I no longer remember how
I earned this sobriquet.
Could've been the volatile
mix of my temperament

and brutal wartime conduct;
could've been my armor,
as displayed upon my tomb.
Could have been my gloom.

Schumann

What *junger Mann* leaves Law,
in violation of his inheritance's terms,
to indulge in *Music*? What mortal flaw

pushes a 19th C. Saxon that way,
from order to billowing desire,
or say, what ethereal fire

found young Robert that day
in Frankfurt when he first
heard Niccolò Paganini play?

"Butterflies," he would later say.
"And the memory of butterflies
carried me away to piano, to Clara."

"The ocean," Clara would correct.
"The ocean and poetry turned
Robert's neck toward the impossible."

"And he ended up in hospital."

King Leopold

For Chris Knerr

Ah Leopold. Leopold!
Belgian King, Congo's captor,
Killer of millions untold,
Veritable human rights
      Velociraptor.

So many Africans left for dead
While you spent your vacation
At a brothel in Hampstead—
Not funny. It was a house
      of flagellation.

You were a Machiavellian,
A pervert, and really quite cruel.
Every right-thinking Belgian
Arrived hours early to boo
      your funeral.

Shostakovich

The long and short of you, Dmitri,
is the long and short of me, though mine
arrives without fanfare. As I sit on my
porch and gaze at the yard my only
music is the double helix of memory
and renewed disdain for other people.

You, with your specs and proletarian
necktie, sit keyboard-stunned, for as you
noted she was a woman desired only
partly, the objective Sofiya reclining
on whatever tacky floral couch
the Bureau had provided.

So was it written, and so, in the heat
of our Soviet season, was it also done—
that march forward through history
and history's illegitimate cousin
Ivan, a drooling amateur, my double,
both horse-like and a clothes horse.

Yet Ivan's keen eye for floral abundance
kept you looking for something you knew
wasn't there yet sensed was real—
or at least real enough to taste
in memory, napping on a rattan
of a wraparound porch distinctly American.

This was your—is our—"muddle
instead of music" and the sound of our
trudging through acres we do not own
toward village lights that have never shone
on us, carrying only our instruments
and, as luck would have it, our papers.

F. Scott Fitzgerald

So tired of people shouting
"F. Scott Fitzgerald!"
I happen to like
Scott Fitzgerald.

The Real Question

The real question being
how will you address these issues
moving forward

so that at the end of the day
you're able to leverage
what you've done

versus what you either have
or haven't succeeded at,
if you will?

Or whether you will or won't,
because time stays for no man;
it merely marks his footprints

as he lopes intelligently
from dune to dune looking, gazing,
via the minimal shade afforded

by an extended salute
so that the hand
becomes a fleshy awning

or hood, the gaze
a pair of Mini Maglites
glowering into a dusky realm.

The Importance of Self-Care
During the Apocalypse

In other news, handbasket sales are skyrocketing,
and so are skyrocket sales, reported skyrocket
and handbasket sales reports earlier this month.

Silver lining? Think again: DriClime polyester
lines a rugged but breathable shell putting this
all-season cagoule at the top of your handbasket

for years to come. "What's in your handbasket?"
goes the popular slogan, though silver and gold
have we none, such as we have we give you—

credit. And the Apocalypse. And a word to the wise:
Take care of yourself. Take a walk, give a hand
job (or jobs), count to 500. You know, Botany 500.

Breathe. The 700 Club. Mile High Club. Fight Club.
Club Med. Breathe (in the air). It's politics
qua politics—it's politics during the apocalypse.

ONE

Hillsborough

Love is not Love which consolation seeks,
but only when on its own two legs it walks
down Margaret Lane in search

of Nothing too beautiful nor no Food too exotic
but only, with this, love, this half
life of his numerous radiating failures,

like the River that goes (yes, wends)
through town under one modern bridge
and past miscellaneous greens, Stars

shining down hopefully on Them, but that's just it:
Hope Kills, says a bumper sticker. And,
It's Not Farm Fresh, It's Not You,

says another. There is infinite Prius,
quantum Volvo, fine rows of such Pickups
as have been carefully mud-speckled,

For when one lives among hunters
one takes what Game one can gather, the saying
goes, be it poached or road-flattened,

so with this, love, this Magic of little roads
converging on our cottage which lies to the West,
full of books, as it is, we have something

if not peace, something if not rain, if not love,
or stars, or the Night Deer wandering through,
Something small and (yes) our own.

My Poetry Went Downhill When You Left

My poetry went downhill when you left,
but it went downhill like a fun toboggan
full of kids wearing colorful caps, just
one of them with a bloody nose from the dry,
frozen air—and a few of them Asian.

Please, that is to say, leave me again,
but this time leave me like you mean it
so my poetry will drop like the New Year's
Eve Ball, glittering, amid drunken cheers,
and explode hilariously in Times Square.

Valentine's Day Poem

How hard it is to be separated
from the one you love;
how much harder to be separated
limb from limb by an orangutan.

Gentler

Men and women should be gentler with one another;
what was it my godmother used to say? *Painfully tender.*

Men and women should arrive and depart together
and without flourish or flattery—just some small banter.

These aren't the gentlefolk you might remember
hearing of I'm describing; these aren't your ancestors.

Men and women in love should appear sister and brother
as much or more than they do ruthless lovers,

flashy, self-conscious, dressed as if by the perfumer,
unwilling to forgive, and in fact, consumed by the anger

that in certain circles passes as love's necessary other.
It's not that, being brutalized, one simply shouldn't bother

to return what has been euphemistically termed *the favor,*
but to say, simply, always remember the heart of your lover

beating full of hope and sorrow, and that life's a river
flowing in both directions, it would seem—forever.

Brothers

I would not be the man I am—
this gentle, recurring presence—
had I not grown up among brothers
who looked out for me always,
who called my BS and laughed
as they walked away punching

each other's shoulders. No,
I wouldn't be this strong-stalked
sunflower, firmly rooted yet
facing skyward, had I not been
planted among similar sunflowers,
whiskery, brave to the breeze,

at ease with themselves:
But I would not be telling these
lies had I not been an only son,
his own shadow, always leaning
forward into something I
didn't understand or want.

White

I grew up white. At the time
I didn't know any better.
White was just white,
and I was just a kid.

Looking back, I think
well what was I thinking?
I had so many options
for what I could have been.

If My Name Were Allison

If my name were Allison
Eduardo Jackaway Markham Spicer
Shillelagh Samothrace Burns
Eliot Commonplace Thoroughgood
Jones Endoplasm Jiminy
Cargill Archer McFleeter
Rebecca Cuthbert Monkingham
Ledbelly Hartwick Shields
Bork Canton Sparkplug McGee
I would go by Allison McGee
or maybe simply "Sparkplug."

A Star in the Face of the Sky

"Multiple ways to avoid stuff but really
no way to actually not do anything,"

says my neighbor Daniel as he, once again,
fails to wash/wax his Volkswagen.

Daniel works for the eldercare police.
He says he's also a novelist and essayist.

"Well, I need to go inside now. Your wife
has been sneaking over at night,"

I say, whimsically, almost profoundly,
my hands extended in a Christ-like welcome,

though no stigmata apparent. "Haha,"
retorts Daniel, occasionally onto me.

I amble into my shady hut, my thatched
domicile, my crappy bachelor lodge

to retrieve a Diet Coke from the oven.
Those were carefree days. Innocuous Dan,

his dull car, our banter, and finally
a baked no-calorie cola, bubbly hot,

the way clues lead into deeper mystery—
a half-tuned television on somewhere.

Poem Composed in 22 Seconds

We think you might be sending
Friedrich mixed messages, Janice.
We'd like you to stop contacting him.
If he needs anything, he'll reach out,
and then you can reach out,
and the sun and moon will reach down
their light, and the rain reach its rain,
and life will go on reaching, imploring,
and feeling its way forward through time;
and that is the end of your picture
book, Janice, here in the middle
of our way. Caught on a rain-lashed
peninsula, poised atop a deck chair,
reading night-time words to a wee one,
both of you drenched, nothing
can get in the way now, Janice.
The future is yours to embargo.

Blue Flashing Lights

Nash & King

Great, there's a drug bust going down
in front of my apartment. Bad neighborhood.
What I mean is there's a sculpture depicting only
drugs' head and shoulders, and it's going down—
crumbling. Bad joke neighborhood. I wonder if
in better neighborhoods there are joke busts
going down in front of nicer houses,
middle managers waddling out in their shark
slippers and tea-pot jammies watching three
cop cars surrounding a corny uncle.
"I was just minding my own beeswax," he'd
chortle, but that'd be it for him: straight to the pokey.
I wonder if people busted for drugs ever
say "pokey," really, or if it's just "the big house"
or "the can." In my neighborhood growing up
we knew "the can" to be one's butt.
"He took it in the can," we'd say. "Cute can
on that new girl," we'd wolf whistle, and stuff.
Those middle managers *are* doing drugs:
that's the irony. And they have real
marble busts here and there in complex homes
that smell of baked goods. No, they don't get
splayed out on the asphalt or remitted to the can.
They're just onlookers searching for an angry fix
at dawn among the hobgoblins of forgetfulness,
hoping to dream the way tender waitresses
dream, of things that are more obviously wrong.

This Morning

This morning gangsters visited.
They said "We want you to join our gang."
They were huddled around my front door
cupping their hands and blowing into them
because it was so cold outside.
They were glancing at each other like,
did we even knock on the right door?
In the street a blue minivan was idling.
"What kind of gangsters are you?" I asked.
"We're from around the way" they said,
"So will you join us or not?"
I must have seemed indecisive because
one of them handed me a business card.
"Call us when you make up your mind"
he said. They trotted back to the van
and got in and slammed the front doors
and slid closed the rear doors till
they clicked which seemed to test
their patience, and as they drove off
I could hear a warning chime as if one
of the rear doors hadn't shut all the way,
so the driver pulled over, and there
was some shouting and fiddling with
the doors, and then they were off
again, the warning chime still sounding,
but I guess they were too proud or angry
to stop a second time to try to fix it.

The Man Who Was Unnecessarily Authoritarian With His Coffee

He said, "You will hold still while I drink you."
And he said, "The matter is not up for discussion."
He said, "After all, I own you. You are my coffee."
Sinisterly he added, "This is not a democracy."
People sitting near him began to stare, became silent,
and they stared through their glasses, their heads
ensconced in turned-up collars, their bodies
swathed in bushy coats, with platinum accessories.
The only sound in the small coffee shop
other than the authoritarian man's voice
was a mild jangling of jewelry and car keys,
for some were getting up quietly to exit, quietly
so as not to interrupt the performance, as quietly
as they could, considering that they were so heavily
accessorized as to be mistaken, possibly,
for metallurgists or German shopkeepers, and so
continued the authoritarian man, barking "Aw!
You are so HOT right now, ha!" and "I shall indeed
drink you down to the botty-bottom of the cuppy-cup,
for when I finish, the barista will fill you back up!"
A small child in the corner raised its hand,
a child with a moon-shaped face and crazy hair,
waited to be called on—but no one called on it.

ZERO

Starbucks

In heaven there's a Starbucks
inside each Starbucks
so that you can be at Starbucks
and on the way to Starbucks
at the same time, etc.

The Love Song of J. Alfred Capslock

HI MY NAME IS T.S. ELIOT CAN U HEAR ME

I'M TRYING TO TEXT U FROM WHEREVER I'M BURIED

I DON'T HAVE A MOBILE TELEPHONE YET SO U HAVE TO BEAR WITH

WANTED TO SHARE A BIT ABT LIFE AFTER DEATH FOR POETS AT LEAST

IT'S NOT WHAT I THOUGHT IT WOULD BE IT SUCKS

I'M NOT SURE WHERE I AM AND I CAN'T GET CAPS LOCK OFF

FOR SOME REASON THERE'S A POSTER OF MATT DAMON IN MY CASKET

WHY I DO NOT KNOW SRSLY THERE'S ALSO SOME INCENSE

IT'S LIKE A SHRINE IN HERE BUT NOT TO ME EXACTLY

I ALWAYS PICTURED THIS AS MORE LIKE A COCKTAIL PARTY

BUT THIS AIN'T THAT SO LET ME JUST SAY IF UR LISTENING

I HOPE U NEVER HAVE TO COME HERE BC IT'S JUST WEIRD

WHAT I REALLY WANT NOW IS TO COME BACK TO LIFE AND SAY
SOMETHING DROLL

I JUST WANT TO BE HESITANT ABT THE BIG QUESTIONS AGAIN

LIKE IS THERE LIFE AFTER DEATH, WHAT IS ART, ETC

BUT I CAN'T EVEN MOVE AND THERE'S NO FOOD

HEY IF U CAN HEAR ME TAP TWICE

UGGH THIS IS JUST BORING SOMEONE PLEASE LET ME OUT

Pride and Prej

It's a truth universally acknowledged
that a single man needs a honey,
especially if said man is rich.

But he must be worth more
than the sum of his money;
and she must not be a bitch.

Hauer You

Hi my name is Rutger Hauer, and this is my cooking channel.
Today on my cooking channel I will make beef.
Great beef starts where you'd least expect.

But before we get into details, let's open a window or two.
I also do have orange juice in the fridge if anybody wants one.
Do you care that I've been in more than fifty

movies and that I am 72 years old and from the Netherlands?
I learned to say American "hello" at very young age.
There is nowhere I would rather be than Iceland, though.

Or that my parents sent me to sea at the age of 15?
Currently running a charity obstetrics clinic in Greenland,
my mind races as I think about what could have beenland.

Two New Jokes

1.

A Jesuit and a wad of paper are walking down the street.
The Jesuit asks the wad of paper what time it is.
No, wait—the wad of *paper* asks the *Jesuit* what time it is.

2.

Three ventricles fall into arguing about which is most important.
"I am, because I have lived a holy life," says the first one.
"No, I am, because I have a large and diverse stock portfolio,"
says the second. "Blah blah blah blah blah," says the third,
seeming, almost to make light of the argument itself.

Litmus Test

Litmus test, litmus test,
why must you indicate
the presence or absence
of acid in a solution?

Why do you go on
day after day,
night after night,
indicating such a thing?

Advice To Children

Children, do not talk to strangers.
If you must, make sure they at least
have candy and that it is good candy.

This is the way of the world.
If strangers have candy or money
you talk to them and try to get some

for yourself. Candy, money, glory;
if a strange man promises you fame,
you do not even need to ask his name.

If a man appears with a strange animal
on a leash, such as a capybara, pet it;
feed it; it wants to lick your hand? Let it.

Remember that the capybara may seem
strange to you, but to Brazilians it is normal,
just as to his mother the strange man

is nothing out of the ordinary.
He is merely her son, and one hopes
she has done her best to raise him well.

Kinderflauten

My feet, at the ends of my legs, do their job.
My face competently presents itself to others.

My hands do their job of grasping fruit
from my neighbor's grove while my eyes

do their job of glancing back and forth.
My legs coordinate with my hips and feet to run

while my heart does its job of beating faster.
My teeth and jaws do their job of masticating,

and my tongue and throat do their jobs, too.
Men and women in town do their jobs.

Children don't do their jobs. They're lazy.
Horrible children who never work!

A child flautist approaches me slowly.
She is trying to trick me into falling asleep!

Truth Or Dare

Playing truth or dare
with God isn't as fun—
he always tells the truth
and has nothing to hide—
nor is it as fun with Satan,
who lies like a rug. Actually,
if you were playing it
with God you might ask
where evil came from.
But even if he accepted
the dare, he's invisible.
And omnipotent. I bet
he'd turn the question
back on you in the form
of a parable about a man
who asks too many questions.

Musical Chairs

In the all-time hardest version
of musical chairs, contestants
sit down, and when the music
starts they stand up and begin
to walk, and all the chairs are
replaced with barrel cacti in large
ceramic pots, and then the music
stops. If you win, you actually
lose. If you lose, obviously,
you also lose. That's why
it's the hardest version.
It's the version they play in hell.

In heaven, musical chairs is fairly
conventional; the only difference
is that when the music stops
the player who forfeits his place
in the circle is the winner.
It is similar to earthly golf.
Having won any game,
however, a player must finish
last in all the others. There are
a lot of games in heaven, actually.
In heaven the rules of golf
are super complicated.

The Difficult History of Rabbits

Coneys, they were once called—
and *kittens* were their young.
Rodents they were believed to be,
though herbivorous, cute,

and gregarious burrowers,
they actually were *lagomorphs*.
Are they pets? To say a coney
is *gregarious* is to note

it roves in vaguely defined herds,
not that it shows up in top hat
and waistcoat twirling its pocket
watch like an overzealous

New Orleans antiques dealer.
To declare such a beast a *bunny*
is to denigrate, at the least;
to encage and kill and then to skin

its fur leaving a long-eared
husk of what it was is worse.
And yet, how irritating
to encounter a *rabbit* knowing

it will merely steal or make
mischief: "A butcher was opening
his market one morning and as
he did a rabbit popped his head

through the door: *Got cabbage?*"
No wonder French monks
once believed them to be fish
and therefore fair for Lenten fare,

as squirrelly as they are
and quick: *unfair game*, perhaps.
No wonder Darwin inquired
into their tendency to tumble

into holes full of magic and rhapsody
and horror: *Are they genetically
disposed to such transport?*
Is therefore a stew or casserole

a mythic hole into which some hapless
trippers have fallen as into
as dream—only to be eaten,
and, if so, *will they awaken?*

CODA

Summer Salt

Sitting at my desk staring off into spices
arranged on a rack nearby: cardamom,
cumin, dark shambles, estrogen.

Peppercorn. Like I don't even know
what sage is, and you do? It's sexist,
and I'm tired of it, and so

is everybody else. We're weary
of being categorized according to arbitrary
criteria like what kind of car we drive.

Standing up, taking it all in with a yawn.
Who has time to canoodle
with an imaginary bank dick

that looks like a cross between Kevin
Spacey and Bert Blyleven? Not eye
will see nor ear will hear,

the famous scripture reads, when He
returns, rendering all this fruitless—
this gesture and these bootless cries.

Succotash

I think good poems—if you can call them good—
are written by people who care so deeply
about everything around them that they're
almost paralyzed. I think those people are like
the proverbial squabs who've inadvertently
dined on arsenic-ridden succotash during
ill-advised raids on one or more seaside
picnics featuring one or more picnickers
attempting to do away with one or more
other picnickers via said deadly corn
and lima bean concoction—wherein the fateful
side dish symbolizes "things of the world"
as tempting fare; wherein arsenic stands for
the mesmerizing hold romantic suffering
exerts on the most emotionally vulnerable;
and wherein squabs are sweetheart kids who,
good with words, deft in action, hyperalert,
weirdly vigilant, and desiring to document it all,
inadvertently eat or lick the most apparently
delectable picnic item upon which they
and their fellow young domestic pigeons (poet
friends) have swooped, and oh buddy, they pay
the price in the form of good poems, and
publishable—fine fodder for literary websites.
They pay the price in the form of a life-
changing delusion that everyone's listening.

Your Poetry

Your poetry, my son, manages the balance
between irreverent and irrelevant
better than any poetry I can recall off the top.

I mean, it's rock solid one moment (when
you compare today's mild rain to your mom)
and then it slips into some inside jesting

the way one squid slips into another squid's ink.
It's as though you're already the best
so there's no sense in besting anyone else

or even in pausing the onslaught of words
just to wonder. Ponder. Wend your way
back on-topic. Your poetry, my son, does all

this and in the space of only a few hundred pages.
It is dandy, irrepressible—a poetics for the ages,
unbeatable if all but unreadable.

In A World

In a world where you
can be anything, be kind
of interesting. Don't
overdo it with the hairdo
and the rumpled blazer
look. Don't keep checking
your Apple Watch.
Drop the act, in other
worlds, such as Saturn.
In a Saturn where you
can't even breathe,
and temps lurk just north
of minus 300 degrees,
be kind. Don't lose
your cool all the time,
because time is on your
side, yes it is. You'll
come running back
to Earth in that
futuristic space-hopping
asteroid-evading VTOL
flying disc you call a "car."

ACKNOWLEDGMENTS

Thanks to the editors of the following publications, in which the poems indicated originally appeared:

Books & Culture: "Making Tea," "The Man Who Was Unnecessarily Authoritarian with His Coffee," "The Real Question"; *The Curator*: "Kinderflauten"; *Education & Culture*: "Capon," "The Difficult History of Rabbits," "Scenic Byway"; *First Things*: "Gentler"; *Journal of Poetics Research*: "Against One Odd," "Chappaquiddick"; *McSweeney's Internet Tendency*: The Love Song of J. Alfred Capslock; *The Missouri Review*: "King Leopold"; *Ohio Edit*: "My Space"; *Oklahoma Humanities*: "Hauer You"; *Prelude*: "A Marketer's Prayer," "Not Feeling So Hot"; *Publishing Genius*: "A Star in the Face of the Sky"; *Smartish Pace*: "Advice to Children"; *The UCity Review*: "Lovesong," "The Importance of Self-Care During the Apocalypse"; *The Weekly Standard*: "Pride and Prej"

ABOUT THE AUTHOR

Aaron Belz has been, recently, a literary critic, stand-up comic, poet-for-hire, UX writer for financial services, consumer-food-product namer, and bicycle-repair-shop owner. He is the author of three previous books of poetry, most recently *Glitter Bomb*, and currently lives in Savannah, Georgia.